STONE and DISTRIC

A Portrait in Old Picture Postcards

by
Roy Lewis

S. B. Publications

This book is dedicated to Dave and Gladys

First published in 1993 by S.B. Publications
c/o Grove Road, Seaford, East Sussex, BN25 1TP

ISBN 1.85770.052 X

Typeset, printed and bound by Manchester Free Press
Longford Trading Estate, Thomas Street, Stretford M32 OJT.

CONTENTS

STONE

SURROUNDING DISTRICT

Front Cover: High Street, Stone

INTRODUCTION

The difficulty in putting together this new volume of Stone and district in old picture postcards has been to make the book complete in itself yet, at the same time, to complement the previous book, *Stone, Sandon and Barlaston* (Brampton Publications, 1988). The cards chosen show many streets and scenes not found in the first volume and, where the same street is shown, it is viewed from a different angle and often at a different date. The brief text below each postcard avoids, as far as possible, repeating facts given in the earlier book. All the cards reproduced date from the years between 1900 and 1940. During these years over 500 postcards were published showing the area covered by this book. Some of these carry the names of national publishing companies but the majority were produced for three local businesses — Thomas Adie & Co, Louis and Philip Dutton, and Arthur Tilley.

The first postcards of Stone were published about 1900 by Thomas Adie, printer, stationer, and bookseller, at 28 High Street, Stone. Adie was not a photographer. By 1905 he had arranged with Francis Frith & Co of Reigate that Frith should take photographs and print cards of Stone with Adie's name on the back. A similar arrangement was made with William Shaw of Burslem and Davidson Bros. of London. By 1912 Adie was advertising 'almost a hundred cards of Stone and district.'

William Shaw, who had a wholesale fancy goods warehouse in Burslem, began producing cards of Stone in 1905. The cards were printed in Germany or Austria and could have either Shaw's or the customer's name on the back. The printing was of high quality and the cards very attractive. Louis Dutton, bookseller, tobacconist and registrar of marriages, at 26 High Street began selling Shaw's cards in 1905 and Arthur Tilley, newsagent and photographer, at 7 Radford Street, in 1906. Tilley also had cards printed from his own negatives in a variety of styles.

At the beginning of 1914 a postcard collector could have found over a hundred different cards of Stone and district on sale locally. Most of these had been printed in Germany and the outbreak of war brought a sudden end to this supply of postcards once old stock had been sold. After 1924 Shaw supplied very few cards of Stone and those available from other publishers were limited in variety.

In 1916 Louis Dutton moved to new premises at 65 High Street where his son, Philip, had a photographic studio. From that date until 1940 cards marked 'Photo by P.C. Dutton' are numerous and provided the best record of Stone and district in the 1920s and 1930s.

Cards produced by Thomas Adie & Co, Louis and Philip Dutton, William Shaw, and Arthur Tilley make up the majority of those reproduced in this book.

The cards are arranged topographically. The reader is invited to start at the south end of High Street, Stone, and walk up to Granville Square before exploring the northern parts of the town. The reader is then led by way of Newcastle Road and Filleybrooks to Walton and the Lichfield Road. This is followed by a wide clockwise sweep through the villages from Aston-by-Stone by way of Yarnfield, Meaford, Barlaston, Oulton, and Hilderstone to Sandon.

Postcards are notoriously difficult to date since publication is often years before the postmark on a card. Dates given in the book are best guesses arrived at by a mixture of internal evidence, postmark dates and a study of postcard publishers.

All the postcards reproduced in this book are from the Lewis collection. Numbers 87 and 88 are reproduced by courtesy of the Earl of Harrowby.

In putting this book together I have been helped by many people who have recalled the scenes on the cards, by librarians who have found books and information, by archivists and historians who have made available the results of their own inquiries. To all of them, too numerous to list by name, I record my grateful thanks. They have made the compilation of this book a journey of discovery and pleasure. I hope that readers of the book will share this with me.

Roy Lewis,
The Oak House,
Crescent Road,
Stafford.

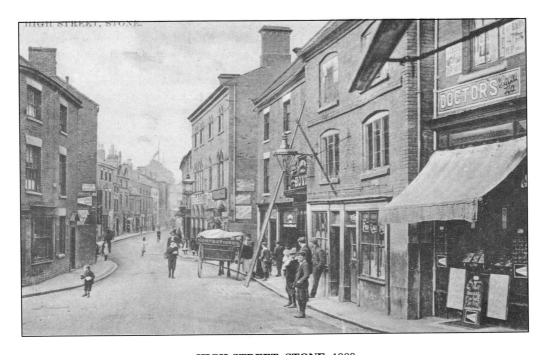

HIGH STREET, STONE, 1908

This view of the southern end of High Street is still recognizable — On the right, the International Tea Stores has a board advertising 'Good Malt Vinegar 3d. a gill'. Next to it are Michael Connor's fried fish shop and William Cregg's barber shop with its striped pole. Beyond that is Anne Norbury's bakery. A narrow entry at the side led to her bakehouse in Scotland Yard from which bread and cakes were carried out in large trays to horse-drawn delivery carts like the one seen on this postcard.

HIGH STREET, STONE, 1924

On the left are the pillars of Cumberland House where the Duke of Cumberland stayed in 1745 when the English army camped at Stone awaiting Bonnie Prince Charlie and his invading army. On the right is the Falcon Inn whose windows and door are now bricked up. On the far right the archway, pulled down long ago, led to a yard where you could leave your horse and trap while you did business in the town. In the nineteenth century it was also the home of Stone's annual Gooseberry Show.

THE CROWN HOTEL, STONE, 1928

The Crown Hotel was the social and business centre of Stone. It was badly damaged by fire in 1778 and rebuilt to a design by Henry Holland which included the large double bow windows seen above. Next to it is W.E. Evans ironmonger's shop (now Castles) which had been extended by 1928 to include what is now Woolworth's. Between the two shops an arch, clearly to be seen behind the parked car, led to Evans' garage at the rear. Today the arch is filled in and used by the Imperial Cancer Research Fund.

THE CROWN HOTEL COURTYARD, 1920

The courtyard lies behind the Crown Hotel. Further back lay a second yard with stabling for horses and space for gentlemen's carriages. There the Mail coaches had once stopped to change horses on their journeys between Holyhead, Manchester and the North, and London. When built, the range of buildings on the left included kitchen, pantry and brewhouse while on the right the arched walkway led to the waiters' boot room and a secure post room where mail bags were kept awaiting the next coach.

HIGH STREET, STONE, 1909

The thatched Black Horse Inn is on the left. Like all the old inns it had a wide entry to a yard at the back. Stone's pigeon fanciers met here. The inn was pulled down in 1954 to make way for a supermarket. On the far side of the inn are the shops of William Smallwood, plumber and decorator; Simpson, high class ladies' draper; Herbert Lawley, ironmonger; and Clarke & Shaw, pawnbrokers, with three golden balls high over the shop. On the right, the bow windows belonged to Joules' brewery offices.

High Street, Stone, No. I.

Photo by P.C. Dutton, Stone.

HIGH STREET, STONE, 1928

Notice the Slow sign on the lamp-post, a sign of the increasing speed of motor traffic. Behind the lamp-post is the shop of Louis Dutton & Son. Louis Dutton sold all kinds of tobacco and pipes and was noted for his snuff. By 1928 the business was run by his son Philip who also had a photographic studio there. Many of the postcards reproduced in this book were sold in this shop. In recent years the building has had its top floor removed and now houses 'The Home and Colour Centre'.

HIGH STREET, STONE, 1914

Compare this view with than on the opposite page taken 14 years later. Notice the difference in the signs on the lamp-post. Louis Dutton's shop is Dr Hartley's surgery and home while the premises on either side are still ordinary houses. The fancy fronted building, now the M.E.B., is the premises of Benjamin Thorley, antique dealer. Next door, the old post office has been pulled down to make way for the white fronted building with the shops of Harry Hague, watchmaker, and William Jacks, photographer.

GRANVILLE SQUARE, STONE, 1905

Before 1903 Granville Square was called Pump Square. Then, to commemorate the coronation of Edward VII, the town pump was taken down, trees planted and a low wall and railings put up round a shrubbery. In the background is the thatched Crown and Anchor Inn and on the other corner of Newcastle Street is the butchers shop of William Blakeman. Ruth, who served in the shop, sent this postcard to a friend at Brocton with the message, 'I suppose you will know me in the doorway'.

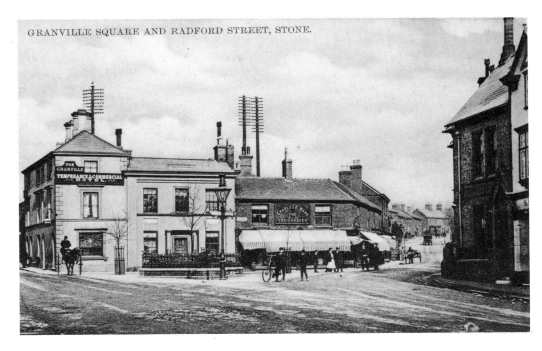

GRANVILLE SQUARE, STONE, 1906

The Post Office was once on the corner of Granville Square and Radford Street. In 1884 it moved into a building next to the District Bank, seen here on the right. The old Post Office building was bought by Charles Babb who opened a drapery shop there. By 1906 Babb had expanded to take in the adjacent shops and the second Post Office building had been pulled down and replaced by the white building on the far right (now Lloyds Bank).

DEPARTURE OF
THE STONE TERRITORIALS
FOR ACTIVE SERVICE. AUG 6.1914.

DEPARTURE OF STONE TERRITORIALS FOR ACTIVE SERVICE, 1914

The Territorial Army was formed in 1908 for home defence if war broke out. When war was declared on 4 August 1914, the Stone Territorials immediately volunteered to serve abroad. This photograph shows them marching from their armoury in the Town Hall along Newcastle Street on their way to the station to join the North Staffordshire Regiment. Newcastle Street has changed completely but the High Street building in the distance (now Lloyds Bank) is still recognisable.

ARMISTICE DAY, GRANVILLE SQUARE, STONE

The War memorial to the men from Stone, Meaford and Darlaston who died in the 1914-18 War was unveiled by the Earl of Dartmouth in January 1921. This photograph was taken by Philip Dutton soon afterwards. It shows a service being held in front of the memorial, probably on Armistice Day. Those with wreaths to lay stand bareheaded in a line across the road and the Stone Military Band is in attendance. Notice that the Granville Temperance Hotel (shown on page 9) has been pulled down to widen the road.

RADFORD STREET, STONE, 1924

This postcard shows another view of the War Memorial. When it was unveiled there was considerable argument about whether the grieving soldier on the monument should have been shown wearing his cap as army etiquette demanded. Behind the memorial is Charles Babb's rebuilt shop with its large 'modern' windows and new style of window display. On the far left the premises of the Meaford & Pirehill Savings Bank, the first bank in Stone, have reverted to being a private house.

RADFORD STREET, STONE, 1918

This view of Radford Street looking towards the town centre is one of many published by Thomas Adie and sold at his stationery shop in the High Street. The view has changed little except that all the railings were removed for scrap during the 1939-1945 War. On the left can be seen the gateposts of Christchurch Old Vicarage and on the right The Royal Exchange with its original bay windows. On the corner of Northesk Street is the shop of Swift & Sons 'authorised plumbers, glaziers and waterfitters.'

POLICE STATION, RADFORD STREET, STONE, 1906

The police station has remained unaltered since 1906 except for the removal of its railings and the ivy on the end wall. The photographer has posed the superintendent and one of the two sergeants outside the entrance while three of the five constables stationed here are spaced out along the street. At that time the normal working day for a constable was 9 hours-without a day off.

POLICE SUPERINTENDENT, STONE

Philip Dutton photographed the Police Superintendent at Stone sometime in the 1920s. Unfortunately no one wrote the name of the sitter on the postcard. It is probably either Joseph Turner or Robert Arnold. The uniform had been adopted in the 1860s. Notice the cap badge with the Stafford Knot and the leather cross-belt worn only by superintendents. By the late 1920s the kepi style hat had been replaced by a helmet in almost every police force except Staffordshire.

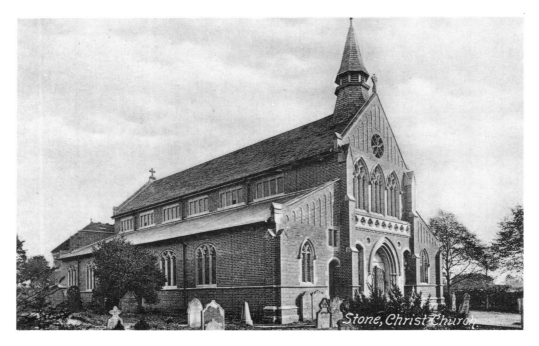

CHRISTCHURCH, STONE, 1905

Stone was divided into two parishes in 1840. Christchurch, the new parish, included not only the northern part of Stone but also villages like Oulton and Meaford. The foundation stone for the new church was laid on Queen Victoria's Coronation Day and the church consecrated in 1840. In 1899 the twin steeples at the front of the church were found to be in danger of collapse. They, and part of the nave, were taken down and the front rebuilt as seen in this postcard.

Stone, Christ Church Schools.

CHRISTCHURCH SCHOOLS, STONE, 1905

The original Christchurch Schools in the Radfords were condemned in 1886 as 'wretched, dark and depressing'. New schools, seen in this postcard, were opened in Northesk Street in 1887. The building, described as 'impressive' in 1887, has remained unaltered outside. The Headmaster in 1905 was Mark Hughes, a remarkable teacher, of whom it was said, 'Most people respected him, some loved him, a few hated him, but no one who attended the school ever forgot him.'

CO-OPERATIVE SOCIETY, KINGS AVENUE, STONE, 1905

Stone Perseverance Co-operative Society was formed in 1875 with Alfred Allen as Chairman and Henry Ravenscroft as Secretary. From the beginning the premises were on the corner of Radford Street and Kings Avenue. This postcard shows the Hygienic Steam Bakery. On a building at the rear can still be read, 'Our Productions are Unequalled'. In later years the shop front was rebuilt with large windows. Today the charitable King's Independent Living Centre occupies the building.

KINGS AVENUE, STONE, 1908

Kings Avenue takes its name from King Edward VII but the street existed before he came to the throne since the earliest house date-stone is 1893. This postcard, taken from Tunley Street, looks towards Radford Street with the Congregational Church spire in the distance. No 26 on the far right was then a shop. The small cross on the pavement outside No 14 was added by William Smith who lived there and sent this postcard to a friend in Leicester.

GRANVILLE TERRACE, STONE, 1910

In 1910 Granville Terrace was reckoned one of the best addresses in Stone. It took its name from Earl Granville, Lord of the Manor of Stone and Foreign Secretary in Gladstone's government. On the left is part of the Congregational Church (now St John's Methodist United Reformed Church), rebuilt in 1886-7 after a disastrous fire, and The Manse, built in 1897. The Sunday School pupils, attracted by the photographers, line the railing which still divide the street from the railway line.

THE AVENUE, STONE, 1910

The earliest houses were built here about 1880 and one still has a brick dated 6.3.82 in its front wall. It was called Gower Street until about 1900 when the name was changed to The Avenue. This view, taken from Radford Street, shows part of the Wesleyan Methodist Church on the left. In the early 1980s the church was pulled down and a row of modern houses built on the site. The alley on the right leads to a back lane that runs behind all the houses.

OULTON ROAD, STONE, 1924

The first shop on the right is William Brinkler's high class grocery cash store. On the far side of the window is an arch wide enough for his horse drawn cart to reach the yard behind the shop. The arch is now blocked. Before 1859 shoe making in Stone was a home-based industry. Then the invention of the industrial sewing machine brought the first shoe factories. In the distance is the first shoe factory built by Thomas Bostock in Cross Street. In 1919 Bostocks became part of Lotus Ltd.

Alleyne's Grammar School, Stone

ALLEYNE'S GRAMMAR SCHOOL, STONE, 1910

In 1889 the Grammar School moved from its unsatisfactory premises in Station Road into new buildings at Oulton Cross 'on the crest of a hill and facing southwest so that there is plenty of fresh air'. There was a hall fitted with desks, an adjoining class room and a headmaster's house. A new block, added in 1908, included the school's first science laboratory and manual instruction room. This postcard shows the new rooms above and the exterior of the new block and 1889 building below.

The Headmaster's House, Grammar School, Stone.   Photo by L. Dutton, Stone.

ALLEYNE'S GRAMMAR SCHOOL, HEADMASTER'S HOUSE, 1916

When the new school opened in 1889 it included a house for the headmaster with space for 16 boarders. The charge was £13 6s 8d a term, or 11 guineas if the boys went home at week-ends. Day boys could dine with the boarders for 3 guineas a term. In 1916 a new Headmaster, H. Malcolm Fraser, had just been appointed to raise standards in the school. Boarders continued to be taken until 1934 when the dormitories were converted into a staffroom and library.

ALLEYNE'S GRAMMAR SCHOOL, SPORTS DAY, 1918

W. J. Harding, Headmaster from 1894-1913, laid great stress on physical training. He inaugurated an Annual Sports Day in 1895, built a gymnasium, laid out the schools first tennis court, and persuaded the Governors to extend the playing field. This postcard shows Sports Day about 1918. The long jump is in progress with straw hatted staff and governors as judges. On the left are the stands for the high jump and in the right foreground the net which was part of the obstacle course.

OULTON CROSS, STONE.

OULTON CROSS, STONE, 1907

When Alleyne's Grammar School was built at Oulton Cross it was surrounded by fields. By 1907 a number of large houses had been built, mostly on the opposite side of the road to the school. This postcard shows some of them. Today the houses are still there but half hidden by trees and shrubs that have matured in their gardens. Notice that the horse and trap is in charge of two young boys.

STONE SPORTS MEETING, 1903

Annual Athletics Meetings started at Stone in 1894. These grew into major sports meetings attracting international competitors. The Staffordshire Advertiser described the 1903 meeting as 'the finest sports held in the country. Such a band of star performers has not been seen in any other place this year'. The highlight was the invitation 100 yards race between R. W. Wadsley (England) and A. F. Duffy (U.S.A.). Duffy won. Notice the pegs and string to mark lanes and the absence of starting blocks.

Old Road, Stone

OLD ROAD, STONE, 1912

This view of Old Road looking towards Stonefield Square was, surprisingly, sent to Gayton from the Hotel du Bois in Paris. Long before the road along the Moddershall valley was built this was the way to Cheadle and Leek. When the valley road was built this became the Old Road. On the right, The Pheasant Inn and the houses beyond it still exist but, on the opposite side of the road, all the houses in the foreground have been pulled down.

STONEFIELD PARK, 1928

Stonefield Par was once the Wakes' Field and before that Pat Ganley's Field. Here the amusements and stalls were set up in Wakes Week and Snape's travelling circus entertained the inhabitants for three pence. Stone U.D.C. bought the field from Joule's brewery, laid out part as a new street called Field Place, and in March 1928 opened the rest as a public park. This postcard shows one of the band concerts given in the summer of that year. The bandstand was taken down after World War II.

The Railway Station, Stone.　　　Photo by Dutton, Stone.

THE RAILWAY STATION, STONE, 1922

The first passenger trains ran into a temporary station at Stone in April 1848. The Staffordshire Advertiser reported, 'Preparations are being made to erect a handsome station in the Elizabethan style. There will be cheese and corn warehouses, shunts for cattle, and coalyards.' The station is an island between the line to Norton Bridge (in the foreground) and the line to Colwich. The central archway led to separate waiting rooms for ladies and gentlemen on each platform. The tower seen over the trees belonged to Bent's brewery.

ST ANNE'S CHAPEL, STONE, 1920

There was no Catholic Church in Stone until Father Dominic, an Italian in charge of the Catholic mission at Aston-by-Stone, began to hold services in the town in 1842. His first sermon is said to have been preached from the back of a cart in a field near the present Convent. Later services were held at 'The Crown' and the house of James Beech. In 1844 James Beech built St Anne's Chapel, shown in this postcard. It still stands in the grounds of St Dominic's Convent.

THE CONVENT, STONE.

ST DOMINIC'S CONVENT, STONE, 1910

After the death of Father Dominic, James Beech invited Mother Margaret Hallahan from Longton to come to Stone. She had been born in London of poor Irish parents and worked as a servant in Belgium before taking vows and returning to England. Mother Margaret Hallahan accepted James Beech's offer of St Anne's Chapel and a site for a convent. She and the sisters began work in Stone, visiting the sick and needy and gaining the respect of all the townspeople even before the Convent and St Dominic's Church were built.

ALTAR OF THE MARTYRS OF STONE, 1903 St Dominic's Church was blessed and opened in May 1854. In the south aisle is the altar of St Winifred with a reredos depicting the Martyrs of Stone. In the seventh century Wulfhere, a pagan King of Mercia, had two sons, Wulfad and Rufin. The sons were converted to Christianity and baptized by St. Chad. In a fit of rage, Wulfere slew his sons. Legend says that their mother buried them beneath a cairn of stones at the place where Wulfad had died — a place thereafter called Stone. The reredos shows the slaying (left) and the baptism (right).

St Mary's Home.
Stone.

ST MARY'S HOME, STONE, 1910
Soon after Mother Margaret Hallahan came to Stone she turned a cottage into a home for a few elderly and incurably ill women. This was the beginning of St. Mary's Home. In 1871 the Home was moved to Elmhurst, once the home of James Beech. The Home was extended in 1893 and again in 1909. On this post-card the centre picture shows Margaret Street with Elmhurst on the right and the later extension on the left. The other views show the Home from the garden of Elmhurst.

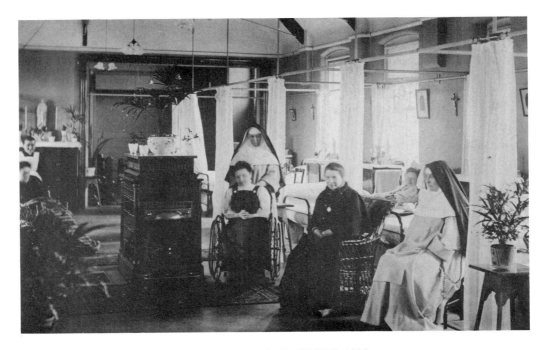

ST MARY'S HOME, STONE, 1905

This photographic postcard shows one of the upper rooms in the extension to St Mary's Home facing Street, as it was in 1905. Notice the numerous potplants.

A BIRD'S EYE VIEW OF STONE, 1907

The photographer set up his camera not far from where the railway bridge crosses the A34 today and took this view across the Trent valley. On the left can be seen St Dominic's Convent and the backs of buildings in Newcastle Street. On the right are the five gables of Joule's Ale Store built in 1881. The central door by which casks were loaded directly onto canal boats is clearly visible.

AIR VIEW OF TONE, 1927

This aerial view can be compared with the bird's eye view on the opposite page. Joule's Ale Store with the Trent and Mersey Canal in front of it is prominent in the centre. In the right foreground is the old workhouse (now Trent Hospital) with the boatyard, wharf and dry dock across the canal. On the left is St Dominic's Church and Convent. Newcastle Street, Radford Street and part of High Street are all easily recognised. Granville Terrace can just be seen in the top left-hand corner.

ST JOSEPH'S HALL RED CROSS HOSPITAL, STONE, 1915

The Stone branch of the Red Cross was formed in 1913 and its members enthusiastically trained in first aid and nursing. In January 1915, as war casualties grew in number, the Red Cross took over St. Joseph's Roman Catholic hall as a convalescent hospital for service men from Stoke and other war hospitals. In May 1918 the demand for beds was so acute, because of the number of men wounded in France, that Stonefield House was taken over as an annexe to the main hospital.

Newcastle Road, Stone.

NEWCASTLE ROAD, STONE, 1905

This postcard shows Newcastle Road looking towards the town centre. On the left are the Victorian houses of Limedale Court with the bearded stone face over the door to number 1. Beyond the houses is the bridge that carries the railway to Norton Bridge and Stafford over the road, and, in the distance, the canal bridge.

The Stone Lawn Tennis and Squash Club now occupies the ground behind the hedge on the right.

THREE ROADS, 1910

This postcard is one of several three-picture cards published by A. W. Tilley in 1910. The top view shows Oulton Road looking towards the town with the tower of Bent's brewery in the distance. The middle view is of Station Road, looking towards the Station yard, with Alma Street on the right. The shops on the right have both been turned into houses today. The third view shows Newcastle Road looking away from the town with Mrs Fanny Newton's shop (now Heath's General Store) at the far end of the first terrace block on the right.

Filleybroors, Stone.

THE FILLEYBROOKS, STONE, 1908

The Filleybrooks, now a double track trunk road, was a quiet country road in 1908. If you travel north from Stone, these five terraced cottages can still be seen on the left-hand side of the road just before the Filleybrooks Stores. In 1908 the end cottage on the right served pots of tea to cyclists and other travellers. A notice 'TEAS' can just be made out on the end wall. Notice the children and adults posed outside their homes.

WALTON, STONE, 1907

This view is unrecognisable today. It shows the view from where the Walton roundabout is today, looking towards Stone. On the left is The Filleybrooks with a signpost directing travellers to Newcastle. In the distance on the right is Elm Terrace and the Stafford Road. On the Filleybrooks corner is Annie Leese's shop with a post box in the wall.

A VIEW OF WALTON STONE

A VIEW OF WALTON FROM THE ECCLESHALL ROAD, 1914

The five barred gate in the foreground is on the corner of Pirehill Lane and beyond are some of the buildings of Priory Farm. Today there are shops where the farm buildings stood and houses cover the fields where old people can still remember picking primroses. Partly hidden by trees on the left is the home of William Evans, the ironmonger whose shop was next to The Crown Hotel. He was well known for the orchids grown in the greenhouses behind his house.

Walton - Stone

WALTON, 1904

This part of Walton has changed little. The bridge is still there although a new road bridge has been built parallel to it. Most of the houses on the left still stand although the lodge to Walton Grange has been pulled down. Walton Grange itself is hidden by the trees. In the distance is Elm Terrace with the main road to Stafford in front of it.

THE CANAL WHARF, STONE, 1925

The canal was opened to Stone in November 1771 amid great celebrations. The arrival of the first boats was greeted with so much cannon fire that a bridge collapsed and damaged a lock. By 1789 Stone was described as 'a little sea-port'. This postcard shows the wharf in Stafford Street. Notice the hand crane behind the canal boat. On the left, behind the trees, was Westbridge House, the offices of the Trent and Mersey Canal Company. In the distance can be seen the frames of two gasometers where the Crown Street car park is today.

ST MICHAEL'S CHURCH FROM STONE PARK, 1920

St Michael's Church was built in 1758 after the tower of an earlier church had collapsed. To the right of the church is Church Street and in the foreground the gate of the level crossing there. The crossing keeper's house with its steeply pitched roof is to the right of the gate. In the distance on the right can be seen the workhouse (now Trent Hospital).

Interior of St. Michael's Church, Stone.

Photo. by P.C. Dutton, Stone.

ST MICHAEL'S CHURCH INTERIOR, 1928

The interior of St Michael's with its galleries and box pews is still typical of an eighteenth century church. By 1886 the church was in need of repair. The Rector complained 'in winter the floor is so damp that it is shameful to ask any person to kneel'. The church was then refurbished and the chancel rebuilt by Lady Forester in memory of her nephew who had been killed at Abu Klea in the Sudan. A new pulpit, seen above, was added in 1926. In 1958 some of the pews were removed to make a children's corner.

St. Michael's Hall and High Street, Stone.

ST MICHAEL'S HALL, STONE, 1911

St Michael's Working Men's Club began meeting in Abbey Street. By 1911 the Club needed larger premises and the hall shown in this postcard was built in Lichfield Street. Outwardly the buildings have changed little since they were built. The gateway on the right led to the Rectory, built in 1758 at the same time as the Church. In the 1870's it became a private house called 'The Priory' because remains of Stone Priory can be seen in the cellars. Today the house has been turned into offices.

LICHFIELD ROAD, STONE, 1914

Road traffic was so light in 1914 that the photographer could set up his camera in the middle of the Lichfield Road to take this picture. On the right, part of the wall still stands but the rest was pulled down when the houses in Claremont Close were built. The houses in the distance still exist and so does the footpath to The Hempbutts beside them. On the left the hedge has been replaced by a grass verge and a sharp dip to Oak Road.

LICHFIELD ROAD, STONE, 1906

This postcard shows Lichfield Road in the opposite direction to the view on page 49. Church Street goes off left in the foreground and the chimneys of the Old Rectory are just visible over the trees. Today Claremont Close, Old Rectory Road, Cedar park and Altona Close have all been built to the left of the road.

On the right the railings have been taken down and the grass verge slopes down to a housing estate.

HORSE LEAPING, COUNTY AGRICULTURAL SHOW, 1906

The Staffordshire Agricultural Society held its first County Show at Stone in 1844. In 1906 the Show was again at Stone in a 'field a few minute walk from town on the road to Sandon.' Among the attractions was horse leaping for a prize of £15. Each horse had to complete two rounds, jumping a hurdle and gorse fence, double rails, a 5 foot gate, a wall, and a water stretch. The rider in this picture is Mr T. P. Hodson of Nantwich.

THE CEMETERY, STONE, 1905

By the end of the nineteenth century both Christchurch and St. Michael's burial grounds were full. Stone U.D.C. bought a four acre site on the Stafford Road to be laid out as a cemetery. On 5 September 1903 the public were invited to join a procession from the Town Hall to the new cemetery but few did so. However, a crown gathered to see the cemetery officially handed over to Councillor Kendrick, Chairman of the U.D.C., on behalf of the people of Stone. This postcard shows the entrance.

THE OLD FOOTBRIDGE, ASTON-BY-STONE, 1905

The road north of the churches in Aston-by-Stone crossed the canal by the bridge seen in the distance and the Trent by a humped bridge on which the photographer was standing to take this picture. The dip between the bridges often flooded and those on foot were provided with the narrow wooden bridge seen here. Today there is a concrete replacement. On the left are the buildings of Aston flint grinding mill, now demolished. The mill house has, however, been modernised and is still occupied.

YARNFIELD, 1908

The centre of Yarnfield was the Labour-in-Vain public house and the Mission Room. The views on this and the opposite page show them from opposite directions. In the view above Highlows Lane and Laburnum Cottage, before its extension was added, are on the left; the horse and cart stands outside the Labour-in-Vain, and the roof of the Mission Room (now St Barnabas' Church) is just visible through the trees on the right. Notice the distant view of fields without a house in sight.

Yarnfield Village, Stone.

YARNFIELD, 1991

In this view the Mission Room is on the left and the Labour-in-Vain on the right. The brook still runs under the road but, on the left, where the ducks are, it is now culverted and even the rails of the bridge have gone on that side. Greenside and Meece Road have now been built on the field beyond the bridge. To the right of the road the ground has been raised so that the wet ditch is now further back. Since 1911 the Labour-in-Vain has had an extension built and a car park added.

THE LATEST MODEL FORD, 1907

In 1907 the Stone Weekly Newsletter reported, 'The speed of the motor car through Stone will soon have to be considered by the authorities. On Sunday one car passed along Lichfield Road at 30 m.p.h. This is dangerous.' This Ford belonged to the licencee of the Labour-in-Vain. His daughter Elsie is behind the wheel. She sent this postcard to Albert with the message, 'I look as if I am just driving over to play that duet.'

YARNFIELD HOSPITAL, 1910

An isolation hospital in a wooden hut had been opened north of the lane from Yarnfield to Stone before 1900. It provided care for those suffering from serious and infectious disease well away from the town. In 1908 the foundation stone was laid of a new hospital on a practical and economical plan by J. J. Chapman of Stone. Today the 1908 buildings, seen in this postcard, are still easily recognisable and even the original wooden building (now a store) still stands as part of Fleethaven Nursing Home.

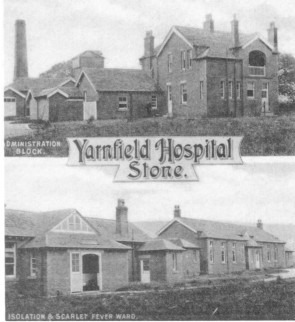

Yarnfield Hospital Stone.

Meaford Hall. Stone.

MEAFORD HALL, 1914

In the eighteenth century the part of the Hall on the right of this picture was the home of Admiral Sir John Jervis. In the 1870s his descendant, Lady Forester, added the clock tower and the wing on the left. She also put in a magnificent Russian staircase. By 1914 the Hall was owned by Lady Forester's nephew. Hilda, one of the maids, wrote on this postcard, 'I am leaving here on Feb 13 as the lady is going away. I am not sorry as it is not a good place. In three months there has been 3 head maids and 4 seconds, so you can tell.'

THE GEORGE AND DRAGON, MEAFORD, 1910

The George and Dragon at Meaford existed at the beginning of the nineteenth century. By the 1880s the inn was in need of repair and a new inn was built by Lady Forester of Meaford Hall. That is the inn shown on this postcard. When the A34 was made into a double track road the inn was bypassed. Today the George and Dragon stands on a quiet loop of road off the A34.

Darlaston Hall, Stone.

DARLASTON HALL, 1910

Darlaston Hall was reached by a long drive from the lodge at the bottom of Yarnfield Lane. In 1880 the Jervis family sold it to James Meakin, a pottery manufacturer, who was still the owner in 1910. Mr Meakin opened the grounds on numerous occasions. St. Michael's Sunday School pupils were usually taken there by horse and cart for their annual picnic and sports day. Mr Meakin provided a drink, a piece of cake and a bun for everyone. It is not known for what occasion the decorations in front of and to the left of the hall were put up.

STATION ROAD, BARLASTON, 1907

Walk up the hill beyond the level crossing and you will see how little this view has change since 1907. The house among the trees on the left is 'The Limes', built by William Jackson in 1893 and still occupied by his family when this picture was taken. In 1950 the Wedgwood Memorial College took over the premises.

BARLASTON SCHOOL, 1924

In 1793 Thomas Mills of Barlaston Hall appointed and paid a teacher whom he provided with a cottage where she opened a school. About 1845 a school was built on the site of the cottage. The school was added to in 1861 and that is the building seen in this postcard. In 1924 the Headteacher was Miss Greatorex, the sister of the village blacksmith, under whom the school flourished. In 1963 the school moved to a new building in Broughton Crescent.

MAYPOLE DANCE AT BARLASTON.
JUNE 20 1912

GARDEN FETE, BARLASTON HALL, 1912
On 20th June 1912 a garden fete was held in the grounds of Barlaston Hall to raise money to equip the new Parish Room near the Green. This postcard shows some of the stalls, the larger refreshment tent, and the donkey rides (on the left). During the afternoon the school children performed maypole dances under the supervision of their teacher.

JOHN THE BAPTIST CHURCH, BARLASTON, 1906

Barlaston parish church was rebuilt in the 1880s in memory of John Blunt, Professor of Divinity at Cambridge, who is buried in the churchyard. Only the mediaeval tower survived from the previous church. Most of the old church furnishings were reused in the new church. This postcard shows the interior soon after a new pulpit had been given in memory of Rev. R. C. Farmer, a former vicar. Note the oil lamps used to light the church. The church was closed because of subsidence in November 1980.

OULTON, 1907

This view of Kibblestone Road looking north shows the centre of the village in 1907. On the right-hand side is the police station with the village constable posed outside. Beyond the police station is The Wheatsheaf Inn, whose first known licensee was William Mills the village wheelwright, and the Brushmakers Arms opened in the 1830s by Gabriel Ludford, a brushmaker.

OULTON ABBEY, 1906

Oulton House has had a varied history. It was built about 1720 by Thomas Dent, a solicitor, and given a new front, shown in this postcard, by John Joule, the Stone brewer. Notice the awkward position of the old chimneys directly above the new front door. In 1838 it became a private lunatic asylum run by Mrs Sarah Bakewell. In 1853 it was sold to a group of Benedictine nuns and renamed Oulton Abbey. The chapel on the left was opened in 1854. The architect was 19-year-old Edward Pugin.

THE LODGE, OULTON ABBEY, 1907

In 1835 Oulton House was bought by the Duke of Sutherland who lived here for three years while major alterations were being made to Trentham Hall. He had this porter's lodge built at the entrance to the house from Oulton Road. The false windows facing the road have now been removed leaving a blank wall.

BLAKEMAN'S GRAVEL PITS, OULTON, 1910

Gravel Pit Field north of the Kibblestone Road had supplied gravel to repair local roads since the beginning of the nineteenth century. In the 1840s the field was owned by Thomas Blakeman, a farmer and butcher, who lived at Rose Cottage on the other side of the Kibblestone Road. About 1900 his grandson, William Blakeman, began to quarry gravel on a larger scale and this postcard shows the workings in 1910. William Blakeman's butcher's shop in Stone can be seen on page 8.

OULTON SCHOOL, 1908
John Ford, Vicar of Christchurch, Stone, raised money for this building in Church Lane in 1863. For 15 years, until the parish church was consecrated, it served as both school and church. After the new school was opened in 1966 this building was pulled down. The children sitting on the wall with their hoops had, according to the school log book, arrived one morning the previous winter 'with wet boots and stockings. So they took them off and a neighbour dried them while the children sat on their toes to warm them.'

Waterwork's Stone

THE WATERWORKS, STONE, 1904

In 1869 there was no sewage system in Stone and many cess pits had been dug close to the wells that were the town's only water supply. In the words of a local doctor, Edward Fernie, 'Water is all more or less polluted and unfit for domestic use'. Nothing was done until 1890 when the waterworks shown on this postcard were opened. Water was drawn from 500 foot deep boreholes near Rockwood and pumped into a reservoir on Red Hill from which all the town was supplied. The works have been demolished but the house on the right still stands.

COPPICE MILL, STONE 1905

Coppice Mill was one of ten mills powered by the stream that flowed down the steeply sloping Moddershall Valley. It was once a paper making mill, then a flint grinding mill, and in 1905 it was grinding calcined bones for use in making bone china. The miller was Henry Shardlow and the mill was often called Shardlow's Mill. The 20 foot water wheel seen in the centre of this picture was in use until the 1950s.

HAYES MILL, THE MILL BANK, STONE, 1910

Hayes Mill lies at the junction of Nicholls Lane and the main road from Stone to Longton. In the early nineteenth century Astbury and Shelley were grinding flint here to add to the clay used in their pottery manufacture. Like other mills it had been converted to grind calcined bone by 1910. It was working as a mill until 1965 and some processing of bone went on until about 1970. The brick cottages behind the mill were built for mill workers.

MOSTY LEE MILL, 1925

This bird's eye view shows Mosty Lee Mill when it was grinding calcined bones for the bone china industry. The mill pond is behind the trees on the right. From there a mill race led to a 17 $\frac{1}{2}$ foot in diameter water wheel on the far side of the mill. The Stone to Longton road can be seen in front of the cottage on the left. The mill stopped working in 1958 but the machinery remained in the buildings. In recent years the mill has been restored and opened to the public.

HILDERSTONE HALL, 1907

Hilderstone Hall was described in the 1870s as 'a neat mansion with plantations and pleasure grounds'. It had been built in the second half of the eighteenth century by Ralph Bourne, a pottery manufacturer, who also established a school and built the church in Hilderstone. This postcard view shows the croquet lawn and garden front of the Hall. Since 1987 it has been a Residential Home for the Elderly.

HILDERSTONE PARISH CHURCH, 1925

For many years Hilderstone was part of the large parish of Stone. In 1833 Ralph Bourne of Hilderstone Hall built the village's first church, ' a handsome Gothic structure dedicated to Christ with walls of excellent stone from Hollington quarry'. This postcard by Philip Dutton shows the church framed by trees. The vicarage can be seen through the trees on the right.

HILDERSTONE, 1905

For this photograph the families from the Village Stores on the left, the Post Office on the right and the nearby houses were persuaded to come out and stand across the road. Notice the horse, with his head in a nose-bag, and a trap outside the Village Stores. Since 1905 the houses on the left have been altered and the arched farm building in the distance pulled down.

HILDERSTONE VILLAGE, 1907

This postcard shows the main street of the village with the B5066 Leek Road on the right. The view is still recognisable although the ivy has been stripped from the houses in the right foreground and the coach house in front of the three-storeyed house on the left pulled down.

THE ROEBUCK INN, HILDERSTONE, 1934

The Roebuck Inn has stood here at least since the early 1830s. The first known publican was Nathan Smith, a schoolmaster by day and an innkeeper in the evening. Later it was kept by Edward Massey, a wheelwright. In 1934 the licencee was John Breeze whose wife can be seen standing in the doorway. Notice the bus timetable on the wall left of the doorway. In recent years the wooden verandah and balcony have been replaced by a new brick entrance.

BURSTON, 1910

The ladies from the two houses on the right stand with their children watching the photographer. In 1910, when this postcard was published, the A51 curved away to the left through Burston. Today the thatched cottage in the distance has been pulled down and the A51 bypasses the village, leaving the old line of the road just beyond the horse and trap.

SANDON.

LICHFIELD ROAD, SANDON, 1906

This postcard of the Lichfield Road shows Stonebench Farm on the right and the gateway to Sandon Lodge in the foreground. On the left, the house with the evergreen tree shaped into rings has been pulled down although its roadside wall remains. In the distance, the Parish Room, built as memorial to the third Earl of Harrowby, can just be seen through the trees.

SANDON POST OFFICE, 1928

In 1928 the Post Office was kept by George Gilbert who was also the proprietor of tea rooms which served refreshments to passing motorists and cyclists. The sign 'TEAS' is clearly visible on this postcard. The houses beyond the Post Office had once been the Post Office and the Police Station. Today they are called the 'Old Post Office' and 'The Old Police House'.

THE SMITHY, SANDON, 1907

This building on the Sandon Hall estate has been a smithy since the early nineteenth century when the brothers John and William Cheadle were blacksmiths here. In 1907 the blacksmith was Roger Downing who also described himself as a wheelwright since he put iron tyres on wheels. In this postcard a pipe-smoking Downing stands in the door way surrounded by wheels, iron tyres, ploughs and other farm equipment.

THE TRIANGLE, SANDON, 1912

This postcard shows the road to Hilderstone at The Triangle. The houses on the right still stand although some of their outbuildings have gone. In the distance is Yew Tree Farm. Today two new bungalows have been built in the field to the left of the road.

SANDON SCHOOL, 1912

Sandon school was founded by the Earl of Harrowby in 1824 and enlarged in 1895. In its early days parents paid 1s -3d per quarter towards the cost of their children's education and the Earl paid the remaining 2s -3d as well as keeping the building in repair. In 1912 the Schoolmaster was David Hicks, who is standing on the far right of this postcard.

SANDON SCHOOL, 1908

On the right is Emma Hicks, the Headmaster's wife, and on the left the pupil teacher who assisted her and might go on to train as a teacher with a scholarship. Most of the girls are wearing a white pinafore — probably their best to have their photograph taken. Most of the boys are wearing either Eton collars or sailor suits.

STAFFORD LODGES, SANDON, 1928

This postcard shows Seven Stars Cottage with its triple chimney on the left and the Stafford Lodges with the gate way and drive to Sandon Hall on the right. In the foreground is the Sandon Estate Memorial to those who died in the 1914-18 War. This was put up in 1920 and , as this postcard shows, originally had the names and inscription carved into the stone plinth. Today the names and inscriptions are on four bronze plaques.

THE 5TH EARL AND COUNTESS OF HARROWBY AND FAMILY, 1937

This postcard, taken outside Sandon Hall in the Summer of 1937, shows from left to right — The Hon Frances Ryder (now Lady Frances Berendt) on 'Pansy'; the 6th Countess of Harrowby (then Viscountess Sandon) on 'Red Ensign'; The Hon John Ryder on 'Kitty': the 6th Earl of Harrowby (then Viscount Sandon); The Hon Dudley Ryder (the present Earl of Harrowby) on 'Rusty'; the 5th Earl of Harrowby and the 5th Countess of Harrowby.

A FOOTMAN AT SANDON HALL, 1914
This footman was photographed outside Sandon Hall about 1914. Footmen's duties included cleaning shoes, making up fires, running baths and sometimes shaving male guests, helping the Butler with the cleaning of glass and silver, carrying luggage to bedrooms on the arrival of guests, laying out the gentlemen's clothes, and assisting the Butler in the dining room.

Other local titles published by S.B. Publications in the series 'A Portrait in Old Picture Postcards':

Bootle, Vols 1 & 2
Liverpool, Vols 1 & 2
Old Bebington
Rock Ferry, New Ferry and Bebington
Southport

Chester, Vols 1 & 2
Crewe, Vols 1 & 2
The Villages of West Cheshire
The Dane Valley

The Lost Villages of Manchester
The Manchester Ship Canal

Aston Villa
Bournville
Pershore and District
The Black Country, Vols 1 & 2
Walsall and District
Wolverhampton, Vols 1 & 2

Aberystwyth, Vols 1 & 2
Chirk and the Glyn Valley Tramway
Connah's Quay & Shotton
Hawarden
Llandudno
Rhyl
Ruthin and District
Snowdonia

Shrewsbury
Wellington

Potteries Picture Postcards
Newcastle-under-Lyme
Stafford and District
Staffordshire Moorlands
Keele and Madeley
The Haywoods, Colwich, Milford and Brocton
Mining Memories
Jarrow & Hebburn

Other local titles available and in preparation. For full details send SAE to:
S.B. Publications, c/o 19 Grove Road, Seaford, East Sussex, BN25 1TP.